This book is dedicated to
NORA - My Mother
1918-1999

Acknowledgements are due to the editors of the following in which many of these poems, or versions of them, were first published:

Breacadh (Ed. Rosemary Canavan); The Bard Of Armagh collections 1996, 1997 & 1998; The Galway, Cúirt, Collections 1996 & 1997, Cúm (Ed. Moya Cannon); Heart of Kerry (Ed. Noel King); The Mermaid's Purse (Ed. Emma Cooke); Podium II, Podium III, Podium IV (Ed. Noel King).

Thanks to RTE Radio One and Radio Kerry where some of these poems have been broadcast and to the Dublin Writers' Festival Poetry Slam, 1998.

Thanks to Maura O'Sullivan, widow of the late Eamon Kelly for permission to adapt some of his stories; and thanks to Jack Lynch for the story behind *The Gentleman.*

Heartfelt thanks to *The Tralee Scribblers Writers' Group* for knocking some shape into a fledgling, though ageing, poet.

Thanks to Bob Jennings, Courtmacsherry Storytelling Carnival and to Siamsa tíre, the National Folk Theatre of Ireland for the launches of this book.

Finally, a sincere thank you to my editor, Noel King.

Both Sides Now

Peter Keane

DOGHOUSE

Both Sides Now
is published by
DOGHOUSE
P.O. Box 312
Tralee G.P.O.
Co. Kerry
Ireland
email: doghouse312@eircom.net

August, 2004

ISBN 0-9546487-3-0

Further copies available at 12 euro, post free, from the above address, cheques etc. payable to Doghouse.

Edited for DOGHOUSE by Noel King

Doghouse acknowledge the assistance of Kerry Group plc.

Thanks also to Tuatha Chiarraí

Cover design: Fintan Wall
Cover illustration: Anna O'Byrne
Printed by Tralee Printing Works, Denny Street, Tralee

Contents

Victim

for Nancy

She notes on the card she completes with a sigh,
triweekly injections in stomach and thigh.
The small yellow pills that she keeps by her bed
fight the terrible pains that she gets in her head.

She is no longer able to rise before ten,
and before eight-o-clock she is tired again.
Medication is sapping her physical powers:
now her day is reduced to nine usable hours.

The housework 's not done but that's not the worst part,
it's seeing her garden that's breaking her heart,
the sight of the flower beds she's tended for years
would reduce any gardener to frustrated tears.

Hobbies she once spent hours keenly pursuing,
she now spends more time in just thinking of doing,
her quilting abandoned, it sits on a chair,
and now she's discovered she's losing her hair.

So how did she end up with all of this strife?
She received a transfusion to help save her life;
but nobody told her on that fateful day,
Hepatitis was part of the price she would pay.

But now things look brighter though it may seem odd,
cause the treatment is working.
It's working! Thank God!

Blind Man Watching

for a vigil in support of East Timor

Sell them guns
Buy their oil
Look away

Build more planes
Sell to all
Look away

It's not our fault
These are *defensive* weapons
Look away

What shooting?
What screaming?
Look away

Who is crying?
Who is dying?
Look away

They need our help
They're looking *our* way
Look away

Just remember
It's not our problem
Look away

From The Inside

it won't work
why won't it work?
i try
i try so hard
it all comes in
it fills me up
why can't I get it out?
important things I mean
i can tell the names of all the cars on the road
i know that the first of May 2020 will be Friday
i just know that
when they ask
i can get that out
that comes out easy
like pressing a button
but when they say *How are you?*
i want to say *Fine!*
but I can't get it out!
all that comes out is *How are you?*
sometimes I see that look in their eyes
especially strangers
it makes me cross
it makes me want to shout *STOP IT!*
but it won't come out
why won't it come out?
then they shake their heads
and say *that* word

what the hell is *Autism* anyway?

Plumbing The Depths

I walk the edge of the tide
On autopilot, mind elsewhere
I skirt pools and rocks
shoes making no impression
on hard-packed silt

It is one of those bright, cold days
which belong only to January
when the day makes amends
for the length and depth of the night

I step on a worm cast
A thumbnail-size crab scuttles away
to dig in at the base of a rock
where the silt is softer

I see where I am
This rock is submerged when the tide is in
A startling thought!

How far out must the tide go
before I can walk across the bay?
Already it seems I might escape
to the other side

That last ripple came in further
I turn and walk towards the dunes
and home
and unavoidable reality

To A 5-Litre Polythene Container

Who dropped you in the river far above
and set you spinning downstream to the sea?
What guided you through pool and fall, to shove
you to the river mouth, same time as me?

I saw you as you hurried past the banks.
I watched as you were thrown from side to side.
I looked on as the breakers caught your flanks.
Then you were tumbled headlong in the tide.

A wave now drives you back the way you came,
but with the backwash off you go once more.
The end of this attempt is just the same,
but still you try to break free from the shore.

At first I thought this would go on for ever,
you'd float around the edges of the bay,
and then, if you succeed in your endeavour,
the turning tide would take you on your way.

But now I know that this is not to be
(nature doesn't ask or offer quarter),
as each wave breaks about you I can see
you settle ever lower in the water.

You do your very best to stay afloat
and though you try to keep an even keel,
you know the sea is lapping at your throat.
My God! I know *exactly* how you feel.

Prophecy

Wind howls.
A diseased wind.
Shredded and befouled leaves
are torn from branches.
Sick rain stabs the earth
injecting itself
deep into the subsoil.
No more,
it can take no more:
The land is surfeited.
First a pool,
then a pond,
now a lake,
spreads across the dying grass.
Small animals
that should have sensed
and fled
the danger
now watch with sick eyes.
Cows at a gate
screaming for the relief
of the milking parlour;
no one to hear.
The people have gone.
It has happened.
Its name
is S E L L A F I E L D.

Omagh

A quiet town,
on a quiet day,
as quiet people,
live their quiet lives.

The quiet is rent by a noise
which will be heard
for generations.

Then the blast.

Shatters buildings,
and lives,
and families.

On the brink of peace the old,
the young,
even the unborn,
are sacrificed for a cause.

This is Ireland.
This is a civilised country.
This is 1998!

May God help us all.

Towards 2000

There's a ceasefire in the country now
No riflemen patrol the town
No barriers close the city streets
It's time to lay old hatreds down

But yet each different Christian sect
Views every other with disdain
And while some people strive for peace
Others work to feed the pain
Most Prods hate the Romans still
And many Romans hate all Prods
And so avoid each others Churches
Like they worshipped different Gods

How this hatred grew and grows
Is difficult for one to see
If you should meet them in the street
You'd find they're just like you and me

They'll take the time to talk a while
Of how their fields are wet or dry
Their failed attempt to give up fags
But still they'll have another try
They'll tell you how they're trying hard
To learn to surf across the net
They'll talk of films and books and cars
Of anything, and yet, and yet

Suggest that we should trust each other
And every spark of reason flies
Their ears close up, their brains shut down
A screen descends behind their eyes

They say there is no other way
You try but they don't want to know
Their minds are closed, their views are set
They hold them, never to let go
For centuries they haven't changed
A product of their homes and teachers
Cemented if they dare to waver
By their churches and their preachers

Now we can only wait and pray
That our besieged, benighted nation
Might change at last if we produce
A new, enlightened, generation

If they work towards a final goal
A lasting ceasefire of the soul

Labels

A label died today.
  It died in Bethlehem,
    or was it Belfast?
      It was shot I think
        or was it a bomb?

No.
  That was a different label.
    Yesterday.
      Somewhere else.
        This one was definitely shot.

They say the bullet entered just below,
  and to the left   of the string-hole.
    A little piece of card fell out
      and fluttered to the ground.

Fortunately, it was only a label.
  If it had been a man,
    or a woman,
      or (Heaven forbid!) a child,
        it would be unbearable.

If the bullet had hit flesh.
  If it had been blood
    and bone
      that fluttered to the ground,
        that would be a different story
          altogether.

But it was only a Catholic,
or a Protestant,
or a Palestinian,
or a Jew.

Just a label.
Not a man.
Not a woman.
Not human.

That's alright then.

Nora - My Mother: 1918 - 1999
written and read as a funeral eulogy

Nora was a sickly babe
Delicate and slow to thrive
Who in the nineteen-eighteen flu
Was the sole survivor out of five

Nora was a strapping child
Growing up when times were hard
Not giving way to richer girls
Led many a fight in her school yard

Nora was a scatty girl
As gay as any in the land
Often known to leave her chores
And hit the town to follow a band

Nora was a blushing bride
Shy, though she would seldom show it
Proud and happy on the day
She wed the man they called *The Poet*

Nora was a loving wife
Unaware of coming pains
Happy when she and her man
Linked arms and walked the country lanes

Nora, a devoted mother
Loved her children, every one
But in those dangerous days for babies
Some were lost but four lived on

Nora, widowed, not yet forty
Faced the future, shed her tears
Couldn't know that their reunion
Would take another forty years

Nora was a mother-in-law
A role that many women dreaded
But she would never interfere
She was far too level headed

Nora changed her name to Nan
Grandchildren gathered at her knee
The pride and love she felt for each
Was in her eyes for all to see

Nora would outlive us all
Full of life and full of fun
Then suddenly the light was dimmed
Her battle over, her race was run

Slow to anger, quick to love
Nora was a faithful friend
Though both of us had many faults
We loved each other to the end

Nora, may God take you on his lap, and kiss you better

Christmas Long Ago

A cowboy hat, a six-gun, and a pooch
every Christmas at the bottom of my bed
I'd put them on and 'round the house I'd mooch
and nineteen times I'd shoot the dog stone dead

Nothing beat the thrill of Christmas morning
I'd wake up half an hour before the cock
then out of bed in spite of Mammy's warning
to see what Santa'd left inside my sock

Maybe chocolate or sweets to spoil my dinner
or - with a bit of luck - there might be fruit
but best of all and bound to be the winner
the inevitable Christmas cowboy suit

Santa must have been the greatest ever
I knew he worked all night without a stop
and the suit he brought, which shows you he was clever
was the one I saw in Matty Quilter's shop

For weeks and weeks we'd roam the street together
sit in bars, play poker, swallow loads of hooch
then travel on no matter what the weather
a boy, a cowboy hat, a six-gun and a pooch

** Pooch (possible corruption of 'pouch') is the word we used for a cowboy's holster.*

** Hooch: slang for cheap whiskey.*

Trauma

I can still feel the pressure
of my Daddy's crossbar
on the backs of my thighs.

I sit on a shiny bentwood chair
smothered by the smell
of rubber, polish and antiseptic.

My Daddy is gone.
I'm too frightened to cry.
A white Nun (I've never seen a white one before)

takes my hand
and leads me up the broad stairs,
rubber soles squeaking on the steps.

I wake up
in a *COT* for God's sake!
My throat is sore,

I want my Mammy.
They feed me ice cream and jelly.
Losing your tonsils isn't *all* bad.

Touching Mary, 1948

Mary Breen is finally at rest
A frail old figure, white, dressed all in brown
'Tis many years since she has looked her best
Now comes the time she lays her burden down
As she lies in peace I hear my Granny say
She was ninety-seven if she was a day

The room is dim, the curtains partly drawn
The candles cast their light across the snuff
The neighbours have been gathering since dawn
In the kitchen now, they've prayed for long enough
So with the adults safely out of sight
A group of young-lads enter the dim light

Now we sit and we stare
At the wispy white hair
And we sample the gloom
Of the snuff-scented room
Then I turn and I say to young Roddy
Have you ever touched a dead body?

Young Roddy says *No*
But I'll give it a go
So nodding her way
I smile and I say
I bet you a ha'penny you won't
He tries, but his fingers say *Don't!*

Mary Breen for long has been my friend
I find it hard believing she is dead
And many times up to the very end
I'd fall asleep while lying on her bed
Though ancient she was never lacking guile
I feel her watching with a quiet smile

Then I challenge the rest
And they all do their best
They'll pick up a dead cat
Or what's left of a rat
But a dead woman's hand is too much
They can't steel themselves for the touch

Now they're looking at me
And it's easy to see
That they don't like to lose
And it's their turn to choose
So even though she was my Granny's aunt
They say *doubles-or-quits that you can't*

They know I'm not the bravest of them all
And think my nerve will fail me in the end
But now they watch me; backs against the wall
As I stroke the hand of my departed friend
And although you may not think it very nice
With my winnings I'll go to the pictures - twice

Treadmill

In school you were top, you collected straight A's
you learned application is something that pays

University years were a means to an end
did you really not notice you hadn't a friend?

At work you were ruthless, you just couldn't stop
you very soon clawed your way right to the top

You're Chair of your club, you've a beautiful wife
your money protects her from problems, from life

She has all she could want, a house like a new pin
yet she seeks consolation in ice cubes and gin

You've an ideal family: two girls and a boy
you made sure they got every conceivable toy

But they've gone off the rails for no reason or rhyme
and complain that they don't get enough of your time

So you tell them they're everything that you hold dear
that you'll all go on holiday sometime, next year

Still you know you won't go you just can't get away
can't put off 'till tomorrow what you must do today

Wealth and power are your aim but you haven't learned that
when you win the rat-race you're still just a rat

Mine

I've often heard you question
why my verse should be so light,
and never shows that life can be
as dark as any night.

You think my work should show more pain
for it to be worthwhile,
not say life doesn't have to be
an endless weary trial.

But I know life's for living,
that I don't have to be drab;
I can show the world is bleeding
without picking at the scab.

You want to see me rend my cloak
and tear out tufts of hair,
as if you value only
my emotional despair.

I tell you there is more to life
than sitting in the dark,
that poetry can shine a light
by striking the first spark.

But you? You want to see my soul,
not happy 'till I bear it.
I say my pain belongs to me,
and no, you may *not* share it.

in the morning light
the mesembryanthemum
opens to the sun

Free Trade

for a vigil in support of East Timor

We've got to sell more arms and build more 'planes
So what if others suffer for our greed
We must fight for our economic gains

Our engineers and salesmen must take pains
To know it matters not what people need
We've got to sell more arms and build more 'planes

We must recruit the liveliest of brains
Most intelligent and ruthless of their breed
We must fight for our economic gains

Our fighter aircraft featuring in *Janes*
Should put our product firmly in the lead
We've got to sell more arms and build more 'planes

Though debt may bind some countries in its chains
With no release no matter how they plead
We must fight for our economic gains

Of war and havoc let us spread the stains
Then sell to both sides, smiling as they bleed
We've got to sell more arms and build more 'planes
They must fight for our economic gains

**Janes Fighting Aircraft: one of several prestigious publications consulted by the arms trade.*

the young butterfly
as it leaves the chrysalis
stops to dry its wings

To Flora

How I love to travel Kerry highways
To see the native plants grow in the hedge
As the seasons change along the byways
New flowers bloom on every bank and ledge
The gentle primrose and the celandine
Will smile to greet me on an Easter morn
Their yellow faces cover each incline
And make me bless the day that I was born
Nature's calendar tears off its pages
Arbutus, foxglove, ankle-deep in peat
Fuchsia filling hedgerows down the ages
With hanging head and nectar, honey-sweet
Before the year is ready to retire
Along the road montbretia catches fire

crack in the pavement
delicate flower pokes through
nature triumphant

Morning

In the waking woodland walking
As the day is just beginning
While the treetop tribe is talking

Fox and badger homeward stalking
Sleeping lovers dream of sinning
In the waking woodland walking

Hunters hunting, hawkers hawking
Night is losing, day is winning
While the treetop tribe is talking

In the distance something squawking
Bees are humming, spiders spinning
In the waking woodlands walking

Feeling free with no one gawking
As the morning mists are thinning
While the treetop tribe is talking

Nearing home my heart is balking
Hearing distant traffic dinning
In the waking woodland walking
While the treetop tribe is talking

dispossessed swallows
rebuilding their little lives
in another barn

Perceptions

They never really saw the man inside
They only saw the markings on his face
It sometimes made him want to run and hide
But a birthmark is no reason for disgrace
At school they called him *piebald* every day
The other boys, the teacher, all the same
The blotches and his glasses seemed to say
He wasn't worthy of a proper name
In growing up the girls he got to know
Though some were kind and others could be cruel
The worst of all were those whose face would show
That someone not like them must be a fool
But then he met the one he lived to meet
She saw the man, he swept her off her feet

daylight weakening
sun escaping from the sky
moon owning the night

The Lost One

for a rally against child exploitation

Skinny one you must work hard today
You will be kept busy I don't doubt
Many men are coming here to pay

Makes no difference what the law might say
With overseers watching all about
Skinny one you must work hard today

Though the room is dim, the walls are grey
The chain around your ankle, short and stout
Many men are coming here to pay

They will come and find you where you stay
And nobody will hear you if you shout
Skinny one you must work hard today

You won't be here forever and a day
By the time you are thirteen you'll be worn out
Many men are coming here to pay

Your parents had to sell you because they
Need food they cannot grow because of drought
Skinny one you must work hard today
Many men are coming here to pay

foxes yawn and stretch
the night has been a good one
spring frosts are their friend

The Old Green Road

The sorrow and the joy, I've seen it all
I've watched events as history tumbled down
I started as a track beside a wall
Before there was a trace of any town
The tramp of many feet defined my trail
I saw the donkey with his loaded creels
As he gave way to sturdy wooden rail
On pony cart, with iron-banded wheels
Then something they called progress came about
New forms of transportation were required
They looked at me and shook their heads in doubt
It wasn't long before I was retired
The brambles grow more strongly every year
Soon comes the time when I will disappear

Camp Thank God

One village with two Churches,
in unity they stand:
Saint Mary's on the hill
prays with
Kilgobbin by the strand.

One of them is Catholic,
most people worship there,
the other Church of Ireland,
a minority at prayer.

Their faithful congregations
wear a path to them each week,
when summer sun is high above
or in the winter bleak.

Their Priest and Rector recognise
each other's sacred roles
of service to their people;
the cure of many souls.

Allegedly they're different
but take a closer look,
for life's important lessons
they are reading the same Book.

One church enjoys sea breezes,
the other mountain air,
yet each can hear the other's bell
ring out its iron prayer.

They've stood for Christianity,
they stand together still.
Kilgobbin by the strand
prays with
Saint Mary's on the hill.

**Camp is a village on the Dingle peninsula.*

The River Finglas

High among the ancient mountains,
seeping, seeping, from the ground;
all around my sister streamlets,
barely infants, can be found.

We are drawn towards each other,
falling, falling, on our way;
fingers touch, we run together,
Finglas sees the light of day.

Life around depends upon me,
drinking, drinking, quenching thirst;
on my bank is room for many,
none need worry who drinks first.

Yet a greater task is coming,
many, many, people wait:
old ones sitting by the fireside,
young ones swinging on the gate.

Gathered in to serve the village,
filtered, filtered, 'till I'm clear;
pumped through pipes to all the people,
all who need me, far and near.

Journey now is nearly ended,
rushing, rushing, making haste;
to the seashore I have travelled,
in my mouth a salty taste.

Erotica

In the distance,
  through the windscreen,
  I see you poised at the roadside;

feet apart,
  hand shading slightly closed eyes against warm sunlight,
  long, light, skirt reaching to your ankles.

Closer
  I raise my hand in greeting but you do not see,
  eyes and mind elsewhere.

Level
  a sudden breeze sculpts your skirt
  to the *exact* shape of your lower body.

Passing
  throat tight,
  blood swamping my brain.

The breeze dies,
but the image is etched on my retina
to return at will:

a pale silk Rodin
which still, sometimes,
keeps me awake.

Dingle Town

Walking
Talking
All the people gawking
Cafe owners chalking
Menus on a board

Meeting
Eating
Food that takes some beating
Uncut moquette seating
How could we be bored?

Clinging
Swinging
While we all are singing
Like a bell that's ringing
Calling in the night

Lying!
Prying!
While the crack is flying!
Who will do the buying!
Handing round the booze!

Blinking
Drinking
With our glasses clinking
And our arms are linking
Everything is right

Glancing!
Chancing!
Everybody dancing!
Like a pony prancing!
Kicking up his shoes!

Waking
Quaking
God! How I am aching
Headache-killers taking
Try to dull the pain

Darting
Smarting
Mind and body parting
Oh what am I starting?
Here we go again!

* *In reading aloud: slow start, gain speed to end of v6, then slow again.*

Dingle Harbour

The fleet is resting, ready now,
moored here side by side,
blue and green and white and red
waiting for the tide.

The nets are mended, now they're stowed
and ready to be shot;
to reap the harvest of the seas
as the finder marks the spot.

The time approaches, all aboard,
the engines warmed and ready,
then round the headland to the sea;
the glass is holding steady.

Another voyage has begun:
their livelihood out there;
the crew gaze at the fading land
and breath a silent prayer.

Now they're on the open sea,
they feel the strengthening swell,
soon they'll reach the fishing ground,
what waits they cannot tell.

A record catch to fill the hold?
A storm and loss of gear?
Still they plough the cold green sea
for year on weary year.

Relentless

The minstrel fills the air with curling notes.
His eyes are closed, head back, and in his hands
The mandolin, the same one that he totes
From town to town on many one-night stands.
I listen, sit in rapt attention, but
The mood is threatened by a thudding foot.

The tone is sweet, the audience responds
Transported on a carpet of his making.
The notes are drops, the songs, so many ponds,
The voyage waits, it's mine just for the taking.
I'm on the brink, I'm leaning forward, but
The spell is shattered by the thudding foot.

The music soars, but now I breathe a sigh.
The spell is broken, all the magic gone.
Then silently I utter my good-bye,
And look around to find the guilty one.
The audience sits still, attentive, but
I see the minstrel's own relentless foot.

The Dingle Train

I am standing at the platform
And I wait the people's pleasure
It's their first time here in Kerry
So they're bound to take their leisure

Now they're walking on the platform
Now they're getting on the train
Now the driver pulls the throttle
I can start to take the strain

As I gather speed my mind goes back
To better times than these
When my whistle woke the countryside
And carried on the breeze

When I travelled the peninsula
With women, men and stock
And the chickens fled before me
And stopped laying with the shock

All the way to Dingle
I would drag the heavy load
Of goods too big and heavy
To be carried on the road

Then back to Tralee once again
Now loaded up with fish
To make sure there was a mackerel
On everybody's dish

But the lorries stole my livelihood
I never got it back
So I'm left to carry tourists
On this little bit of track

Now I see the other platform
For the thousandth time this year
And this story now must finish
'Cause my journey ends right here

Reading aloud: v 1 & 2 very slow, gain speed until v8, then slow to a stop.

Parade

This is the route
and here we stand
waiting to hear
the big brass band
This is the day
when we have planned
to cheer the greatest
in the land
Now as I squeeze
my Daddy's hand
it's getting louder
isn't it grand
This is no music
soft and bland
This isn't bogus
This isn't canned
Now they are marching
on the strand
leaving their footprints
on the sand
Now the music
is softer and
I ease my grip
on my Daddy's hand
glad we're here
and as we stand
we heard the greatest
in the land
Now we can barely
hear the band
as off they march
along the strand
we hear the music
softer and...

A Tribute to Eamon Kelly: 1914-2001

I fell under the spell of Eamon Kelly, *The Seanchaí*, in the 1970's when he brought his one man shows; *Bless Me Father, In My Father's Time* and *A Rub of the Relic*, to Tralee. I was only recently returned from England and hungry for the taste of the Ireland I had known some twenty years before. I saw his live performances as often as I could and listened endlessly to his audio tapes until I knew every pause, aside and *Ahem*! of his delivery.

Eamon was so much the consummate storyteller that it was years before I realised that he was not *just* a storyteller but a great actor playing the part of the *Seanchaí* so brilliantly that he defined the role for the nation.

He had, and still has many imitators of all ages who deliver his stories, complete with all the pauses, asides and *Ahems!* that I recognise from my tapes. I have seen many of these perform at venues around the country and the similarity is uncanny, but I have rarely heard any, with the honourable exception of storyteller Pat Speight, acknowledge the source of their material.

This made me wish that I could perform his work like them so that I could acknowledge his authorship. Sadly, I am not a storyteller, but after Eamon's death I sought permission from his widow, Maura O'Sullivan, to translate his stories into verse. She agreed, and the first four of my adaptations appear on the following pages.

As you read, please remember that all of the verse, and some of the words, are mine; but the stories belong for ever to Eamon Kelly, *The Seanchaí*.

Peter Keane, Tralee, 2004.

Doing The Rounds

On the morning of the first of May, approaching eight o'clock,
the milking done and bonamhs fed since woken by the cock.
The people left their cottages with smiles for one and all
and travelled down the mountain like a human waterfall.

You know that they were passing by the pounding of the brogue,
while some men came on horseback with their women up *cúlóg*.
They came to kneel and pray around their local holy well
and gave rise to many stories that a man might want to tell.

The roads were lined with beggars who had taken up positions
to expose their various ailments with most gloomy dispositions.
Here a blind man with a placard, there a scrawny withered hand,
or a grossly swollen goitre; now the biggest in the land.

They'd call down Heaven's blessing for a penny, which was cheap,
(If He didn't hear them calling God would have to be asleep).
But woe betide the fella who put nothing in the hat,
he'd be sentenced to eternal fire and that, they say, was that.

Now there'd be tents around the Well where you'd find women selling cake,
or toffee apples, lemonade, whatever they could make.
Another tent sold goat's milk that was topped up from the still,
it would straighten any backbone, 'twas the cure for any ill.

But none would touch a drop no matter how the vendors tried
'till the prayers had been recited and the body mortified.
Some men were so determined for the spirits to appease
that they rolled their trousers up and did the rounds on their bare knees.

Which reminds me of a man you might have heard of from Rathmore.
He thought he might get married, he was nearly fifty-four.
He found a girl and courted her and everything went well,
the wedding day approached and he was ready for the bell.

But on the fatefull day his auld alarm-clock left him down,
he woke with just an hour to go and three miles from the town.
He dressed and raced across the fields as quickly as he could,
but first he rolled his trousers up to save them from the mud.

Arriving at the church he saw the people all inside.
He rushed up to the altar to be with his lovely bride.
He smiled politely at the priest who answered with a frown,
and hissed at him quite sternly *Will you let your trousers down!*

He thought of all the people there and glancing at his bride,
he blushed as red as beetroot as he stood there at her side.
The people all smiled at him just as if he was a clown,
while the Priest hissed even louder *Will you let your trousers down!*

The trouble was his cronies had been telling him for days
that in some religious ceremonies the Church had changed its ways.
The Pope had called a Council that had altered some details,
but he wouldn't know the changes 'till he got up to the rails.

Now the Priest was looking at him like a half-demented jinnet,
the smiles on people's faces getting broader by the minute.
Then finally he found his voice and all that he could say
was *If you don't mind Father, can we do it the old way?*

But back here at the Holy Well the penitents were praying,
some mumbled low while others made it clear what they were saying.
Some barefoot and some on their knees did circuits while they prayed
and others found a soft spot to kneel down and there they stayed.

While some men rolled their trousers up to keep them from the dirt,
the way the women managed was removal of the skirt.
These they placed upon the wall in many-coloured drifts
and went about their business in their well-worn flannel shifts.

One man, the most devout of all to see him do the rounds,
would close his eyes and beat his breast and utter moaning sounds.
So great was his devotion to the Spirit and its call
that he didn't see a bright blue skirt had fallen from the wall.

He kept on moving towards it with his knees all caked in dirt
'Til a man who knelt beside him said *Hey you! Lift up the skirt!*
I won't the fellow answered in an agitated hiss
It's because of doing that, that I am here now doing this.

The same man, they called him Paddy, was a barber of some skill,
said to be the best in Ireland since the time of Columcille.
Every morning he'd be seen before he opened up his shop
as he set off to the Palace with his razor and his strop.

There he did what he was best at in his own decisive way,
you see the shaving of the Bishop was his first job every day.
He did this every morning, did it seven days a week,
'cause a Bishop can't be seen if he has stubble on his cheek.

But Paddy had a weakness as you might have guessed no doubt,
mostly he was sober but on some days he'd 'break out'.
And so it was one Saturday his hand was far from steady,
he watched the Bishop through a mist as he was getting ready.

When he had done the Bishop took the mirror from its place
and looked at all the spots of blood that covered half his face.
Then the Bishop said *The drink 's a curse* his foot upon the fender
You're right M'Lord the barber said *It makes skin very tender.*

* *Cúlóg: on the horse's bare back behind the saddle.*

Mossy Malley And The White Bucket

It was nearly half way through September
Mossy Malley was heading to town
When his wife called him back to the kitchen again
And said with her usual frown

When you've finished your fun with your cronies
And heard all of the tales they can tell
Remember to buy me an enamel bucket
A white one to use for the well

So in town when he'd finished his business
And drained his glass to the last drop
He drove with the mare and her ageing flat car
To the Hardware and Drapery shop

Now the mare was inclined to be flighty
And he wasn't sure what he should do
In the end he just left her there standing alone
Sure he'd just be a minute or two

He went in and picked up a bucket
And went to the counter to pay
Then he saw by the crowd that was already there
He'd be stuck for the rest of the day

He was keeping an eye through the window
To see if the mare was alright
But when he'd been there for ten minutes or so
Something caused her to bolt with the fright

Forgetting he still had the bucket
Mossey ran out of the shop
Quickly followed by Maher, the owner (& Sons)
Who was shaking his fist shouting *Stop!*

They quickly surrounded poor Mossy
And Maher, his voice like a sting
Grabbed hold of the bucket and said to the crowd
There is too much of this sort of thing

Mossey tried to explain to a Peeler
A red-headed, pimply, youth
But he was ignored 'cause in those days, as now
Money talked and, what 's more, told the truth

About thirty days after this happened
He got his 'Whereas' in the post
To appear before old Justice Johnson himself
A far kinder Justice than most

He knew just by looking at Mossey
That he never intended to rob
But because of the evidence offered in Court
He still had to fine him ten bob

But the worst part of all was the moaning
And nagging he got from his wife
And when she saw his name in the papers that week
He knew he'd be martyred for life

And of course 'twas the talk of the neighbours
The best thing to happen of late
'Twas the subject of all of the talk to be heard
On Sundays around the Church gate

For fear of some more indiscretions
She told him, in pious alarm
From now you are confined to Barracks my boy
You mustn't set foot off the farm

For weeks he endured isolation
Because she wasn't talking to him
And as it moved into December he knew
That his prospects were looking quite dim

But then on the run-up to Christmas
He thought he at last saw his chance
I have to go in for your present, you see
He told her, avoiding her glance

Alright, you can go in next Friday
And buy me that silver-backed comb
It's in there in Hilsers, the jewellers shop
But mind you're not late coming home

It was well after dark when she saw him
By his flashlamp approaching the gate
She flung open the door and demanded to know
As to what it was kept him so late

He said I *went in to confession*
And to kneel down and say a quiet prayer
But when I got into the Chapel at four
Nearly half of the Parish was there

She said *Did you mention the bucket*
That you stole from the Hardware and Drapers?
Don't be stupid he told her *Of course I did not*
Sure he saw about that in the papers

The Umbrella

Larry and his missus heard 'twas their turn for the Station
So they set to work on planning it and showed no hesitation
Now the Stations are held sacred dating back to penal times
But with several small differences in these more modern climes

Where he once said mass in field or wood as timid as a mouse
The Priest now comes with ceremony to say mass in the house
And all the nearest neighbours will arrive in ones and twos
To bow the head and bend the knee and then hand up the dues

Now Father John, the parish Priest, accustomed to prosperity
Was known for his demeanour 'cause it bordered on asperity
Though to callers at the Presbytery he's all courtesy and ease
And doesn't make you feel that you should scramble to your knees

I was told that by a fella who I only knew as Harry
His girl was from another place and making plans to marry
He wanted a letter of freedom, saw the Priest write out and blot it
Though as things turned out thereafter he was sorry that he got it

When Station day arrived the neighbours gathered for the Mass
The morning, soft and misty, put a sheen upon the grass
Then looking down the bohereen, a man shouted out *He's here*!
A rush into the house, nobody wanted to be near

But Larry held his ground, not that he wanted to be there
As Father John came mounted on a sixteen-hand black mare
But what the Priest was holding fairly addled Larry's brain
'Twas a black roof - like a mushroom mounted on a walking cane

Good morning father Larry said and reached up for the reins
The Priest then headed for the house, stepping 'round the drains
Then Larry tucked the mare up warm and dry inside the stable
And hurried back towards the house as fast as he was able

The people lowered their gazes as the Priest approached the door
Though none of them had ever seen an umbrella there before
By the time they all looked up, because with him they were so shy
He'd reopened the umbrella and had stood it up to dry

Everything proceeded in the way it was expected
Confessions heard, the Mass was said, and then the dues collected
The Grace of God was in the house, you'd sense it in the mood
And the Priest was in the neat front room demolishing the food

The men stood in the kitchen all admiring the umbrella
And all of them proclaiming 'twas a handy little fella
You could stick it on the roof if ere a hole came in the thatching
Or prop it on a barrel where the goslings might be hatching

Having polished off his breakfast Father John came back again
And looked out through the door as he addressed the waiting men
How's the morning doing, is it still as it began?
Oh it's cleared away already Said one forward sort of man

I've much to do the Priest replied *I'd best be on my way*
The men stood back respectfully not knowing what to say
They bade the Priest *Good morning* then with countenances gay
'Cause the bottle would stay hidden until he was on his way

Larry brought the mare out and she quietly took her load
Then he fell in step beside her as they headed for the road
They'd just got past the gander when the Priest cried out *Oh my!*
Please go back for my umbrella, I might need it bye and bye

Back down the bohereen our Larry scurried like a mouse
He hardly drew a breath 'til he was back inside the house
He grabbed at the umbrella and he turned towards the door
But what happened next near had him falling over on the floor

He knew the mushroom should go out the same way it came in
But no matter what he did the thing would not go out again
He tried this way and that but he could not reduce its size
The neighbours stood and looked at him with pity in their eyes

He said *We'll just take off the door, we'll lift it from the hinges*
They all stepped forward as one man, this was no time for whinges
With the door off the bacáns and the result the very same
The next thing they decided was to get rid of the frame

It wasn't very long before the frame lay on the ground
He tried it once again while all the neighbours stood around
No matter how he turned the thing the hole was still too small
There's nothing for it Larry said *We'll have to knock the wall*

Now Father John was puzzled when he heard all the commotion
Though what might be the cause of it he didn't have a notion
Afraid that his umbrella might be damaged by some blackguard
He turned the mare around and trotted back into the haggard

He got down from his saddle and he walked towards the door
And the sight that met his eyes was like he'd never seen before
When he arrived poor Larry was about to swing the hammer
What is all this? he asked and Larry answered with a stammer

If I can shift that c-c-corner stone there isn't any doubt
With a l-little bit of juggling the m-mushroom should go out.
Just stifling a laugh the Priest gave out a stern command
Stand back! They did, and he took the umbrella in his hand

Now Father John plus overcoat was what you might call 'wide'
'Though his passage through the door was watched by everyone inside
In a flash he closed the brolly, headed out into the rain
Before any one could notice it he opened it again

Imagine their surprise when he walked over to the mare
The black roof on the walking stick held proudly in the air
He swung into the saddle with a style they'd never seen
And, with a final nod, he trotted off down the bohereen

When Father John had left them they all gathered in the room
The bottle opened, passed around, soon lifted any gloom
They sipped as they discussed it for the best part of an hour
Then Larry said *Say what you like, they have the bloody power!*

* *Bacáns: crude hinges*

The Looking Glass

I have often wondered how the women managed
Until somebody thought up the looking glass
And the fellas seem to spend as much time at it
Especially on a Sunday before Mass

Now one man never knew that they existed
He lived out in a backward sort of place
If he'd known he'd make a better job of shaving
Instead of taking skelps out of his face

When C.I.E. announced a cheap excursion
To the City, that's a place he had never been
He went off in a spirit of adventure
Determined to see all that could be seen

The city was much bigger than expected
In a cafe he ate spuds and mutton chops
With more pony-traps than he had thought existed
But the strangest of the lot was all the shops

In one big shop he saw a pile of purties
All sitting there and shining in the light
He picked one up and slowly turned it over
Then saw a thing that made him doubt his sight

He stood there feeling very hot and bothered
He felt that he was getting in a lather
'Cause he could see the thing that he was holding
Was a picture of his late, belovéd, father

He gazed in admiration at the 'picture'
How ever had they got a hold of that?
But there couldn't be a doubt it was his father
Right down to the angle of his hat

He said *Tell me girl, where did you get all these from?*
From London, she replied with haughty air
Well, unless he passed through on his way to Heaven
I never knew my father had been there

Sure it only cost a trifle so he bought it
And slipped it in the pocket of his coat
To admire when he thought no one else was looking
A circumstance his wife was quick to note

Of course he never told her of the picture
She'd never been his father's closest friend
If she knew he had his picture in his pocket
Her nagging would have sent him 'round the bend

Although she wasn't noted for her patience
She knew that she would have to wait her chance
To see just what it was he kept admiring
And on that day she'd make the devil dance

One day his neighbour's chimney went on fire
He heard the shouts and shot out like a rocket
His Missus saw the coat he'd left behind him
Like a ferret she was straight into his pocket

She looked into the mirror in amazement
And then she caught her breath, she fairly spat
Who's this woman he spends all his time admiring?
An auld hairpin, and an ugly one at that

It must be someone he met in the city
I should have known that he'd go off the track
As for the name of this auld Dolly Varden
I'll find that out as soon as he gets back

She put the looking glass back in the pocket
And waited for her husband to return
She'd make him pay for causing all this trouble
She'd show him she was not a one to spurn

When he returned she launched her great offensive
What's this picture that you carry in your pocket?
Some fancy-woman you met in the city?
It's a wonder you don't keep it in a locket

That's no woman! That's a picture of my father!
In a dress? She asked and grabbed her coat and hat
And called back as she headed down the footpath
We'll see what the Parish Priest says about that!

Now when the Priest heard what she had to tell him
He said *I really can't believe my ears*
I know him as a pious, sinless, Christian
He has her picture! She choked out between her tears

Well if that's the case I'll have to take some action
Alright my child I'll come home with you now
And find out what he has to say about it
We'll settle this today, you have my vow

And when the Priest had landed in their kitchen
He said *Listen here to me now my good man*
Just hand me out that picture of a woman
And we'll sort this out as quickly as we can

The husband was alarmed at this instruction
But knew he didn't dare to answer back
He quickly took the mirror from his pocket
And turned it over to the man in black

He snatched it from the man without a *Thank you*
Held it up before his face so he could see
Then laughed, and said *Aren't ye pair of eejets,*
That's the Parish Priest ye had here before me

Touché

Three friends at university
Were wont to meet each day
In a cafe on a corner
Just to pass the time away

This day was no exception
So they turned up one by one
To find their favourite table
Had been taken by a Nun

They stood and talked it over
As they waited in the queue
By the time they got their food
They knew exactly what to do

Determined that they wouldn't sit
In any other place
They thought they'd make her move
By bringing blushes to her face

So they sat down right beside her
And to converse they began
The tone that they adopted
It was strictly man to man

Said the first *Some of our neighbours*
Are still treating us with scorn
'Cause my folks were only wed six months
The day that I was born

That's nothing said the second
As he sucked in both his cheeks
My people only beat the stork
By barely seven weeks

Said the third *I'm glad to hear that*
'Cause to tell you I was dreading
I'm off tomorrow to attend
My Dad and Mother's wedding

They watched the Nun's reaction
As the seconds trickled by
Until finally she raised her head
And looked them in the eye

And then she asked quite calmly
In a voice as smooth as silk
Would one of you three little bastards
Kindly pass the milk?

Enthusiast

Now Edward is a curious man
Well into his allotted span
Each evening finds him in the park
Happy in the semi-dark

By day he checks his chosen site
Then lurks there in the fading light
To startle each approaching smasher
The fact is: Edward is a flasher

For years this hobby he's pursued
Well aware that it is rude
But standing there, his knees like jelly
Is better than just watching telly

Sometimes all consuming rapture
Hampers his escape from capture
But still he gets a certain buzz
When he is picked up by the fuzz

There was a time some years ago
When certain ladies in the know
Would creep along from tree to tree
Just to see what they might see

But so long has he pursued his goal
That time's begun to take its toll
And now it's plain for all to see
He's not the man he used to be

Some cheeky girls when they pass by
Now boldly look him in the eye
But that is better still by half
Than those who only look and laugh

Each winter when the winds grow higher
He wonders if he should retire
But then as spring is drawing near
He sticks it out for another year

A Christmas Letter Home

Dear Mum,

When I said I'd like a sweater I did not mean one like that!
With green and purple zigzags and a matching knitted hat,
And a drawstring round the waist with great big bobbles on the ends.
Do you think I'm going to wear it and be slagged by all my friends?
The bright red tartan slippers are a very cheerful sight,
I'd be quite glad to wear them but they're just a little tight,
I know that they're the same size as you got for uncle Lew
But he is four-foot-ten and I am six-foot-bloody-two!
The pipe rack from young Johnny must have really left him broke
It does look quite expensive, what a pity I don't smoke.
The roller blades that Granny sent must also have been dear,
I'll put them with the pogo-stick I got from her last year.
The after-shave from auntie Joan will help to keep out rats,
I walked down to the gate and now the garden 's full of cats.
Now I hear the carol singers, they're the worst I've ever seen,
They can't tell God Save the Weasel from Pop Goes Our Gracious
Queen.
And yet I'll ask them in to share some fruit cake and a beer,
Because I still believe that Christmas is the best part of the year.

Your loving son,

Peter.

Beneficiary

I'd been left an old house by my cousin
She'd lived to a hundred and five
I was told that she'd been a collector
And hoarder when she was alive

Her collection she left to the Nation
Her cash to St. Vincent de Paul
What was left then when I took possession?
Some junk in the attic was all

I decided to check what might be there
And found in reward for my toils
An old violin in a suitcase
And an interesting painting in oils

Suspecting these might have some value
To Christie's I hurriedly went
The receptionist, seeing my items
Passed me on to an elderly gent

He examined my treasures minutely
Then checked them all over once more
He said he'd not seen a Picasso
And a Stradivarius together before

When it came to the question of value
He said, stroking both of his chins
Stradivarius was useless at painting
And Picasso made crap violins

Motormouth

Professor O'Brien is an expert you know
A prince of debaters and much in demand
He will hold your attention and never let go
And his audience sits in the palm of his hand

He is willing to speak any where any time
He delivers his views with amazing velocity
He will speak on the merits of lager and lime
With conviction and characteristic verbosity

He could tell you how Jason discovered the fleece
He can talk the whole night on the state of the nation
He would speak about horses or donkeys or geese
Or the merits and drawbacks of canine castration

He would keep you enthralled on the strength of the pound
Or the benefits which we have gained from the Euro
He'd discuss the best way to get stereo sound
Or the most secret contents of some lady's bureau

He's been called to the Dáil to address the T.D.s
On planning and ex-territorial bankers
He told them that men who used people like these
Could best be described as incurable - onanists

It had been his proud boast now for many a year
That with ease he could keep any audience charmed
'Till a lady's club, chaired by a lively old dear
Suggested a subject that had him alarmed

To prepare in his mind he just cleared all the decks
Then arrived in good time at the prestigious venue
For the subject they'd asked him to speak on was sex
Still they fed him quite well from a very good menu

Then he got to his feet and he looked round the hall
And addressed all the ladies in words they still treasure
There is only one thing I must say to you all
Madam Chairman, dear ladies, it gives me great pleasure
Thank you

She Who Hesitates...

Now some people speak very slowly
But it isn't quite what you'd call sloth
It could be a problem in just finding words
Or constrictions surrounding the throat

One such was a young man called Sammy
He spoke always at a snail's pace
An effect which was magnified time and again
By the agonised look on his face

'Till his colleagues in exasperation
Said *Can you not increase your speed?*
The time that you take when you're talking to us
Makes it really quite hard to pay heed.

Young Sam knew they spoke out of friendship
And never intended offence
So he took a deep breath, and he marshalled his thoughts
And made this speech in his defence

Now I know that you think I speak slowly
That my rate of speech couldn't get slower
But my sister, just eighteen months younger than me
Believe me, she speaks even slower

It was on a fine evening last Summer
As she went for a stroll in the park
Enjoying the scents and the sounds of the place
She walked through the gathering dark

When an elderly person approached her
And blatantly made her a bid
And before she could say that she wouldn't do that
She did

Reading aloud: Last three stanzas to be read as slowly as the reader can bear

The Go-Between

Long ago and far away the Israelites did roam
They walked across the desert, they were looking for a home
They numbered many thousands, were an oddly diverse band
And without the law to guide them things got very out of hand

Now Moses was their leader and was wearing to a frazzle
He threatened to resign 'cause he was fed up with the hassle
So he clambered up a mountain for a pow-wow with his boss
Who sat inside a burning bush and Moses was quite cross

Now look here God he shouted *we are running round like fools*
If we're going to get anywhere you must give us some rules
Now take it easy, Moses boy The Supreme Being replies
Here are 23 Commandments, that should open up their eyes

So he went back down the mountain with the tablets in his hands
And he summoned all the leaders of the different family bands
They studied the commandments, they consulted with their peers
They held a referendum and the whole thing took them years

When all of this was finished they put Moses in a fix
Instead of twenty-three Commandments, they only wanted six
So he went back up the mountain, he was gone for seven days
Until finally they saw him reemerging from the haze

Then they gathered all around to hear the message from the bush
As Moses started speaking, well there was a deathly hush
He said, *First, here is the good news, He has cut them down to ten*
Unfortunately the bad news is - adultery is still in

Killer-Thriller

The first body, wearing a brown leather jacket,
Its head still enclosed in a large Corn Flakes packet,
Was found by police who, without hesitation,
Said *Clearly the cause of death was suffocation.*

The next was a young lad preparing for school,
Each morning he ate what his Granny called gruel,
And, although on his jumper there wasn't a speck,
He was drowned in a bowl of his own Ready Brek.

The third was a lady aware of her figure,
Determined that she wouldn't get any bigger
Through the window they spotted her, stretched on the floor:
There were traces of arsenic in her Country Store.

The last was an athlete intent on his training,
Each morning he ran, be it sunshine or raining,
Then early one morning he ran out of luck,
And was killed by a runaway Weetabix truck.

Newspaper reporters were hungry for news,
They hounded Inspector O'Dea for his views,
He said *It's just like you might find in a thriller,*
This is clearly the work of a cerial killer.

Bear Hunt

A hunter went to Russia to bag himself a bear
He'd heard that it was possible to do that over there
He landed outside Moscow and quickly made his way
To get himself a permit to start his hunt next day

The man in charge of hunting had a problem 'cause he knew
That the only bears in Moscow were residing in the zoo
I'll tell you what we'll do he said *I'll have to ask around*
To see if someone knows somewhere a bear might still be found

That night he told his problem to his brother-in-law Vlad
And as things worked out after he was very glad he had
'Cause Vlad told him a story and it caused his heart to leap
The circus had a tired old bear and it was going cheap

The next day it was all set up, the bear was put in place
The official met the hunter with a smile upon his face
He took the lavish fee before he handed out the permit
Said *A big bear has been sighted near the hut of an old hermit*

He didn't tell the hunter how the bear had been acquired
That in fairness the poor creature should be decently retired
So the hunter set out cheerfully as all good hunters should
Checking details on his map, he travelled deep into the wood

In the early afternoon - he had just answered nature's call
When he saw the hermit's hut with a bike leaning on the wall
Then, just as per report, like a colossus standing there
In the middle of the lane he saw a bloody great big bear

The hunter took his rifle, aimed directly at the beast
All the moving parts of it were adequately greased
But as he squeezed the trigger something hit him on the knee
He knew not what but 'cause of it his bullet hit a tree

The startled bear looked at him, he thought his time had come
It headed straight towards him and his heart beat like a drum
But it only knocked him over as it galloped down the lane
Then the bear jumped on the bike and it was never seen again

Sharp Practice

A man in a sweat hurried into the Vet
With a rabbit wrapped up in a sheet
He'd had a job trying to stop himself crying
As he carried his pet down the street
He was only just able to stand by the table
While the Vet looked and then shook his head
Then he stifled a sob while the Vet did his job
And told him *The rabbit is dead*

He said *Though I regret the demise of your pet*
And I'd hate to suggest something shoddy
If you leave it with me I'll be happy to see
That someone takes care of the body
Said the man, his lips tight, *That will not be alright*
He has been my companion for years
Now the one thing I crave is he has a nice grave
And it might help to stifle my tears

Said the Vet *That's 0 K, I'll arrange it today*
In the smartest pet burial grounds
These are people I've checked, he'll get all due respect
But the cost will be fifty-five pounds
The man looked at the bunny, said; *I don't mind the money*
But there is just one thing that I dread
That my little friend Clive might be buried alive
Please make sure that he really is dead

Saying no more the Vet went to the door
And brought in a Labrador dog
The dog went to the rabbit as if it might grab it
While the rabbit lay stiff as a log
And then from its nose to the tips of its toes
The Lab poked it with his big paw
Then he finished his stuff, gave a little sad *woof*
While the owner looked at him in awe

Very soon after that the Vet brought in a cat
It was tabby and sleek and well-fed
It looked all 'round the room as if sensing the gloom
And finally nodded its head
Then carefully paced and without any haste
It examined each bunny detail
Without making a sound it looked all around
Then left with a small mournful wail

The Vet said *Enough, those two both know their stuff*
Your bunny is tucked up in heaven
Now I've checked the amount so here's your account
It's four hundred and three, fifty-seven
The man looked aghast but recovered quite fast
How could it be that much? he cried
The Vet smiled to himself, took a book from the shelf
Then turned to the man and replied

You said you'd pay around, I think fifty five pound,
For a plot that was peaceful and sunny
But that was before you asked for a lot more
And Lab tests and Cat scans cost money

How The Other Half Loves

Her Ladyship lay in her Boudoir
She had only just wakened from sleep
She thought of last night's consummation
So much better than just counting sheep

She looked at her sleeping companion
How the light caught his, now greying, hair
And she wondered if he'd ever leave her
A thought that filled her with despair

The morning peeped in through the curtains
'cause the darkness of night had now fled
And very soon Perkins, the butler,
Would bring her her coffee in bed

A small sound escaped her companion
Like a tiny bird safe in its nest
Then he turned and, one could say by instinct
His hand found its way to her breast

But by now she had fully awakened
And aware that her throat was quite parched
Soon Perkins would bring her warm croissants
On a napkin all perfectly starched

He'd devoted long years to her service
Had done all that her household required
But soon he was due for his pension
What would she do when he retired

She'd tackle that problem tomorrow
But soon on her coffee she'd sup
Then she turned to the figure beside her
And said *Perkins, it's time to get up!*

Hurler On The Ditch

After almost two thousand years mooching 'round heaven
Saint Peter now felt like a change
So he had a wee chat with an angel called Kevin
As they stood by the golf driving range

It has been quite a while said Saint Peter *you know*
Since I witnessed a good game of soccer
Shall we challenge the fellas residing below?
Wouldn't that be a bit of a shocker?

I'll find you a Captain the angel replied
He is just over there by the statues
He was back in a minute and there at his side
In long knickers stood old Stanley Matthews

Saint Peter said *Stan, you're just the right man*
I want you to pick me a team
Then work on your training, make out a good plan
I want them to play like a dream

The challenge was issued, the challenge was met
The caterers worked on the menu
The pitch was in limbo, the best they could get
'Cause they wanted a neutral venue

To ensure He saw everything as it transpired
God had his throne fixed on a swivel
Then for broadcast he had the whole stadium wired
While the angels they cheered like the devil

'Twas a hell of a match, when it came to half-time
The score was still stuck at nil-all
Then God switched on his mike, sipped a vodka and lime
And spoke in a dismissive drawl

I have never seen anything like it He said
Neither side seems to know what it's doing
As for you lot He turned to the angels, who fled
You shouldn't be cheering but booing

Our side are like cripples, they miss easy goals
All their attempts are just farces
And the rest should have stayed where they were in the coals
With hot pokers stuffed up their - noses

Now at this Stanley Matthews got rather uptight
And went off in search of Saint Peter
Who said *Don't get upset, it will all be alright*
In a voice that just couldn't be sweeter

It is always like this each time we have a game
Though I know it makes you feel uncumfy
See the trouble we have, and it's always the same
Is that God thinks that He's Eamon Dunphy

Poetry?

There once was a time
when poems would rhyme
and they told of a deed or disaster.
Now that time is the prize
poems are cut down to size
and poets must work a lot faster.

No more six hundred horses
running their courses
charging the mouth of the cannon.
No more Bridge of Athlone
felled by sinew and bone
or heroic deeds outside Dungannon.

Rhyming 's now out of style
it has been for some while
'cause the effort required is alarming
just write down what you like
and some modernist tyke
will assure you he finds it quite charming.

For a subject you must
hunt around in the dust
because uplifting thoughts are forbidden
and for greater allure
you must keep it obscure
it is best if the meaning is hidden.

If success you pursue
the one thing you must do
is ensure that your poems don't scan.
So my best course of action
if I must join this faction
is to try to squeeze as many words into the last line of my poem as I possibly can!

Bon Appetite

Two cannibals sat down to dinner
To a pot of comedian stew
The fatter one said to the thinner
Does this stuff taste funny to you?

Encounter

It chanced in mediaeval times two travellers did meet
Each on their separate journey in the pleasant Summer heat
The lady was a Holy Nun though she was worldly wise
He was a court Jester, grotesque and low in size

She wore her robes with dignity, took care to ward off smells
He, a living parody, wore Jester's cap and bells
They walked along together then, each with a separate goal
He, to his new master   she, to save her soul

They travelled through the greenwood till a river barred the way
She said *I fear to cross it, on this side I'll have to stay*
I may be ugly he replied *But strength I do not lack*
No need to fear the river, you may cross it on my back

So he hoisted her aloft and started out across the flood
She knew she was defenceless but it saved her from the mud
They hadn't got half way across when he came to a stop
His body shook, he staggered, and she feared that he might drop

Then he flung back his monstrous head, his laughter filled the air
Desperate now that she might fall, she clung on in despair
She cried *Why do you laugh?* He replied in tones meticulous
I've just seen us for what we are: Virgin on the ridiculous

Competition

The gas station had a promotion
That had people queuing with cheques
A contest, to enter you just spent ten bucks
And the prize, if you won, was free sex

The promotion had lasted some time now
When Mo and Ed drove into sight
They had heard of the prize that was offered
And the thought had their jeans feeling tight

They filled up and paid at the counter
The man took their cash with a smile
When they told him they wanted to try for the prize
He stood there and thought for a while

He said *Right, now I've thought of a number*
It is somewhere between one and ten
But remember if you guess the wrong one today
You can enter again and again

Mo and Ed looked at each other
Neither knew quite what to do
Then having discussed it they settled for five
The man replied *Sorry, it's two*

As they drove away from the station
To their cabins way out in the sticks
Mo turned to Ed, who was driving and said
I think this competition is fixed

Ed said *No, I don't think he's cheating*
'Cause that wouldn't be very nice
But the reason that I can be sure about that
Is my wife won it yesterday - twice!

Quizmaster

You're all very welcome to our Table Quiz,
As Quizmaster you'll find me a bit of a whiz,
Now if you're all ready we'll get down to biz,
I'll be back from the bar in a tick.

So - who was the first man to fly 'round the moon?
What was the first record made by Pat Boone?
When did the dish run away with the spoon?
Oh! And another red wine for me, Mick.

Who was the actor that played The Quiet Man?
What is the capital of Pakistan?
Who wrote the play Lady Windermere's Fan?
One more glass there to keep the throat slick!

How many air miles from here to Hong Kong?
Did Dominick Behan record Annie's Song?
To which U.S. State does George W. belong?
And another red should do the trick!

How many legs on a three-legged chair?
What livestock do school children breed in their hair?
Why have you all got that look of despair?
No! A white - the aul' head 's a bit thick.

What kind of sighs do they have in Siam?
How many Ps would you find in a pram?
No! I'm not half a thunk as you drink that I am!
Oh God! I'm off home, I feel sick.

Samaritan

One man approached another in the street
And said *Could you tell me the w-w-way*
To the R-r-railway St-st-st-st-station
I must get to C-c-cork without delay

The other stood and never said a word
Made no attempt to offer a reply
And far from giving any kind of help
He wouldn't even look him in the eye

Fearing he had been misunderstood
The first man thought he'd better try again
He said *If you p-p-please, I'm in a hurry*
I really must c-catch the t-t-train

Once again the other didn't speak
With lowered eyes, stood staring at the ground
When the first man once again asked for his help
He just whistled to himself and looked around

A lady who was standing close at hand
Overheard this strange one-sided conversation
And pitying the traveller in his plight
Explained where he would find the Railway Station

As he set off along the noisy street
She raised her voice and added to the din
She asked *Couldn't you have helped that poor man out?*
He said *And get my f-f-feckin head kicked in?*

Sixties Swinger

Now Johnie and Joe were the best friends you know
Every evening would find them together
They would travel the land on the heels of the band
Never caring a fig for the weather

To dance through the night was their greatest delight
They were well known in each country hall
But 'twas Johnie who'd dance like a man in a trance
While Joe stood with his back to the wall

You see late in the day when the cows had their hay
The two lads washed their curly red locks
Then as if heaven bent applied lashings of scent
But Joe never once changed his socks

So each night at the dance in a mood for romance
With the girls not inclined to say *No*
Without straining his voice John would nod to his choice
But no one came within ten feet of Joe

Now you might think it odd or a bit of a cod
That John never told his best friend
But he was fond of the kid and was afraid if he did
That this long valued friendship might end

Then one night at a dance he at last got a chance
There were girls there in beautiful frocks
Joe asked *What must I do to get partners like you?*
He said *Go out and take off your socks*

So after a while Joe came back with a smile
Like a gigolo fresh in from France
With his mind in a whirl went to many a girl
But he still could get no one to dance

At a quarter to two in a terrible stew
Joe was driving the car like a rocket
John asked with a small cough *Did you take your socks off?*
Yes I did, they're here in my breast pocket

Raiders

Two ships appeared on the horizon
Sails squared off and oars beating time
The sun caught the well burnished helmets
A picture you could call sublime

But the year was eight-hundred-and-fifty
And this wasn't a mission of peace
'Twas the Vikings out looking for trouble
Like Jason had searched for the fleece

Together the ships reached the shoreline
And nosed themselves onto the sand
And over the sides poured the raiders
Each with an axe in his hand

As one man they stood to attention
As the Officer walked up and down
He squinted and searched the horizon
And looked at the sun with a frown

Because one of his ships was still missing
And he couldn't start raiding without
It finally appeared 'round a headland
To be greeted with many a shout

Its sail drooped and sagged at the mast head
Its oars had no rhythm at all
When it stopped the crew jumped from the sharp end
Well, they didn't so much jump as fall

They limped and they crawled towards the others
They tried to stand in a straight line
But they couldn't and stood there all droopy
You'd think they had been at the wine

Then the officer spoke to the first crew
On this raid the burning's your job
Then he ordered the next crew to pillage
And he turned to the dishevelled mob

But before he could give his instructions
With a voice that was heavy with pain
The leading crew member cried *Mercy!*
For God's sake, not ravishing again

Robin's Rest

Robin Hood lay supine on his pallet
His life was approaching its end
Little John and Maid Marian sat by his side
His sweetheart and very best friend

He said *Dear friends, I know that I'm going*
I can feel a great weight on my chest
But before I set out on this ultimate voyage
I want to make one last request

Please give me my bow and an arrow
Place them right here in my hands
Then I'll shoot the arrow as far as I'm able
Please bury me where ere it lands

Maid Marian found him an arrow
And Little John gave him his bow
It pained them to see such a great man as Robin
Finally stricken so low

With his last gasp he pulled back the bowstring
And loosed it before they could blink
'Twas a pity his finger slipped at the last minute
And they buried him under the sink

Souvenirs

The two of them had come up for the match
Their team had won, and so they'd stayed the night
Now they were setting out their train to catch
And neither of them was a pretty sight

They knew they'd be in trouble with their wives
When they got home, 0 God! how they'd berate them
For drinking and carousing in low dives
They'd buy a gift! A sure way to placate them

They wandered through the shops in muddled state
Looked at Leprechauns and cheap brown plastic thrushes
Then realising it was getting late
They settled for two lavatory brushes

They bore their gifts away in fuddled pride
With little time to spare they caught their train
As it rocked upon the rails they nearly died
And of course they swore they'd never drink again

They met again, the way that these things go
In a little pub they called The Burning Bush
One said *There's something I would like to know*
How did you manage with that lavatory brush?

Just fine the other said, *Why do you ask?*
He replied *We find it awkward to control*
We've decided for so delicate a task
We're going back to using toilet roll

The Gentleman

'Twas a quarter past two of a Sunday
With the pub getting ready to close
When into the bar walked young Thomas himself
With a black-eye, and a stitch on his nose

Now Thomas he isn't the brightest
And his arrival that day was quite late
And the look of him had us all wondering aloud
How he'd got himself into that state

For a while he just kept his own council
He wouldn't say divil a word
'Till the heat and the booze set his larynx to work
And this was the story we heard

I was sittin' at Mass there this mornin'
Meditatin' I spose you might say
But the truth is my mind had been ramblin' around
I was thinkin' of Match of the Day

'Till we arrived at the Our Father
When as I stood up on my feet
I saw in the pew just in front of my own
As nice a girl as you could meet

She was blonde and about five foot seven
With a figure to make your heart hum
But I noticed the cloth on the back of her dress
Was tucked in the crack of her bum

Immediately I was distracted
The prayer I completely forgot
With the sight of the shine on that wee piece of cloth
That was tucked in the cheeks of her bot

Then I thought that it might be uncumfy
And that really it was quite unfair
For to leave that magnificent rump on display
With the other lads startin' to stare

So as quiet as I could I reached forward
To below where the cloth was so full
And catchin' it in between finger and thumb
I gave it a delicate pull

As the week passed the eye changed its colour
From black to a deep purple stain
It had finally settled to yellow and green
When it came 'round to Sunday again

We were sitting discussing the hurling
And tempers were running quite high
When in through the doorway walked Thomas again
With another, and matching, black eye

Everyone in the bar was struck speechless
To see poor Thomas looking so pale
So we sat the man down and we got him a pint
And he told us the rest of his tale

He said *It was just like last Sunday*
I was sittin' enjoyin' the Mass
When I noticed the woman in front of my pew
Was the one with the marvellous ass

And when we stood for the Our Father
Just like it happened last week
The colourful cloth at the back of her dress
Was held, you might say, cheek-to-cheek

I stood there and tried to ignore it
Concentratin' with all of my might
But the man on my left just stood there starin' at it
Like a rabbit that 's caught in a light

Then calm as you like he leant forward
Like a man in the grip of a drug
And taking a hold of the back of her dress
He gave it a bit of a tug

But I knew that she didn't like this
And I feared that she might make a din
So before she could turn and do anything rash
I reached forward and tucked it back in

Based on a story by actor and storyteller, Jack Lynch

The Literalist

The little boy was late for school
The teacher said *Look here, you fool*
What stopped you getting here on time
You know we start at half past nine

The boy looked down - took off his cap
Explained that there'd been a mishap
The trouble was his father's horse
Fell down a hole concealed by gorse

He ran to neighbours round about
Who came in answer to his shout
They promised him they'd come right quick
And never fear, they'd do the trick

And so they came with beam and rope
To lift the horse, the only hope
But tugging made the animal fret
So he'd been sent to fetch the vet

Said father *Save the horse I beg*
The vet replied *You see that leg?*
It can't be fixed, no use to frown
I'll have to put the creature down

The Teacher's anger ceased at that
He gave the boy a friendly pat
Did they shoot him in the hole? he said
No Sir, they shot him in the head

The Optimist

The couple's young pet sow had come on heat
An occurrence which had not occurred before
They knew to have some bonhams round her feet
They'd have to get the creature to the boar

Now normally they'd take her to McNiff
His boar would do the job without much fuss
But their car was off the road; a broken diff
And they knew they couldn't take her on the bus

They pondered for a while on what to do
The way to McNiffs house was flat and narrow
Said the husband *With a little help from you*
I think that I could wheel her in the barrow

It wasn't quite as easy as they thought
To settle the sow down and spread the load
But they gained the equilibrium they sought
And so they tottered off along the road

They reached the boar, who greeted her with glee
Upon his face they clearly saw a smile
Said McNiff *Come in and have a cup of tea*
We'll leave those two together for a while

Before they left for home they told the farmer
That on matters such as this they were quite thick
They said *Although your boar is quite a charmer,*
How will we know if he has done the trick?

He said *I'll tell you how to judge the lass*
Tomorrow you go out and look around
If she's pregnant she'll be nibbling at the grass
If she isn't she'll be pawing at the ground

'Twas early morning when he sauntered out
To see if that first mating had succeeded
From what he saw he knew without a doubt
That once again the barrow would be needed

By now they had the knack and it was quick
The barrow soon was carrying its load
Then once again the porker did the trick
And soon they trundled back along the road

Next morning well he nearly lost his life
He looked out quite amazed at what he saw
He scratched his head and went to tell his wife
That their pet sow must have some kind of flaw

She said *You'd think that she was on the pill*
D'you think we'll ever get that one to farrow?
He said *If it's up to her I'm sure we will*
She's out there sitting in the bloody barrow!

* Bonhams (pron. *Bonavs*): Piglets

Well Met

'Twas on a train the Rabbi met the Priest
And nodded quite politely as they sat
They didn't know each other in the least
But very soon they settled down to chat

They talked about the weather and the day
About their daily work within their flocks
And as they travelled smoothly on their way
They gazed upon green fields and jutting rocks

After they had chatted for a while
And were running out of subjects for their talk
The Priest turned to the Rabbi with a smile
And said *Tell me, have you ever eaten pork?*

The Rabbi looked about in some surprise
His body-language clearly said *Defence!*
Then saw the smile in his companions eyes
And knew the Priest intended no offence

Well now he said *Without exaggeration*
And since it is no great or mortal sin
Just once, but may I say in mitigation
That day I had had rather too much gin

Now it's my turn said the Rabbi to the other
And you realise I don't intend to vex
So although I know you wouldn't tell your mother
You can tell me now, have you ever had sex?

The Priest now looked about in some confusion
To check if there was any likely hearer
Then seeming to have come to a conclusion
He beckoned to the Rabbi to come nearer

O.K. he said *Since you've told me your tale*
And I suppose that it is just fair play
Before I joined the Church I met young Gail
And I 'knew' her in a 'Biblical' sort of way

The Rabbi smiled and sat back in his seat
And said, *I bet you she was quite a smasher*
The Priest replied in tones quite bittersweet
'Twas a bloody sight more fun than any rasher

The Dangers Of Satan Worship; Especially At Christmas

They told him Satan worship
Was the best way to succeed
That the Diabolic Powers
Would give you everything you need
So he rented all the films
And watched them on his D.V.D.
He believed what he was watching
Was the only way to be
He'd heard of covens practising
This blackest of the arts
Believed that joining in
Was the best way to maiden's hearts
Convinced that Satan worship
Would help him to have his way
With many ripe young ladies
(Ones he didn't have to pay)
Determined he would find a way
His evil vows to make
He studied all the books
And so he made his great mistake
'Cause alas he was dyslexic
So although he didn't plan-ta
Through some misunderstanding
He sold his soul to Santa

Pastoral

The ancient shepherd rested
as he looked upon his sheep
Many hours would pass
ere he would lay his head in sleep

He watched his faithful dog
who held his charges in a clearing
dependant on his master
always stayed within his hearing

He gazed across the mountain
where for years he'd grazed his stock
his pale blue eyes could see
the weaker members of his flock

The time was when he would have culled
the weaklings at their birth
but he had come to see
that every life had its own worth

He knew that at this altitude
birdsong was rarely found
but now a chirping filled the air
he recognised the sound

It was one of those sweet interludes
on which all shepherds thrived
His missus on the mobile phone:
The headage cheque 's arrived